The Complaint and the Answer

SHIKWA & JAWAB SHIKWA

THE COMPLAINT AND THE ANSWER

The Human Grievance and
The Divine Response

MUHAMMAD IQBAL
Translated by Abdussalam Puthige

The Other Press
Kuala Lumpur

Published by
The Other Press Sdn. Bhd.
607 Mutiara Majestic
Jalan Othman
46000 Petaling Jaya
Selangor, Malaysia
www.ibtbooks.com

The Other Press is affiliated with Islamic Book Trust.

Perpustakaan Negara Malaysia   Cataloguing-in-Publication Data

Muhammad Iqbal, 1877-1938
      Shikwa & Jawab Shikwa: The Complaint and the Answer:
      The Human Grievance and the Divine Response / Muhammad Iqbal;
      Translated by Abdussalam Puthige
      ISBN 978-967-0957-00-5
      1. Urdu poetry. 2. Poets, Urdu.
      I. Puthige, Abdussalam. II. Title.
      891.43915

Printed by
SS Graphic Printers (M) Sdn. Bhd.
Lot 7 & 8, Jalan TIB 3
Taman Industri Bolton
68100 Batu Caves, Selangor

The Author
Allama Muhammad Iqbal
(1877-1938)

Sir Muhammad Iqbal (1877-1938) was a great poet, philosopher and a leader of the twentieth century. He was born in Sialkot, Punjab. His ancestors were Kashmiri Brahmins who had embraced Islam some three centuries ago. After completing his early education in Sialkot, Iqbal moved to Lahore, where he completed his graduation at the Government College of Lahore. He earned his master's degree in philosophy and English literature at the Oriental College. He joined the Government College of Lahore once again, but this time as a lecturer in philosophy, history and literature. He started writing his poetry in Urdu at a very early age. His work was noted for its depth and versatility. During his days in the

Government College of Lahore, he was in touch with stalwarts of literature like Sir Thomas Arnold.

In 1905 Iqbal travelled to Europe to pursue further studies. He qualified for a scholarship from Trinity College in Cambridge, England, and obtained a Bachelor of Arts (BA) degree in 1906. During the same year, he was admitted to the Bar as a barrister by Lincoln's Inn. Later, Iqbal moved to Germany and earned his PhD degree under the guidance of Friedrich Hommel, from the Ludwig Maximilian University of Munich in 1908. "The Development of Metaphysics in Persia" is the title of his doctoral thesis.

Apart from England and Germany, Iqbal visited some other countries in Europe and met many scholars, writers and political leaders. In Spain, he visited Cordoba (Qurtubah) and offered prayers at the historical Masjid of Cordoba. This visit is said to have had great influence on him. In Italy he met Mussolini. During his stay in Europe, Iqbal began writing poetry in Persian.

In 1908 Iqbal returned to Lahore and started practicing law. At the same time he devoted much of his time to literary activities and played an active role in politics too. He was a member of Anjuman Himayat Islam. In 1919 he became the general secretary of this powerful organisation. He was conferred knighthood in 1922. In 1927 he was elected as a member of the Punjab Legislative Assembly. He presided over the annual session of the Muslim League in 1930 and attended the Round Table Conference held in London to frame a constitution for India.

Iqbal has written seven books in Persian and four in Urdu.

One of the most important themes evident in the works of Iqbal is *khudi*, translated as "individuality," "self," "selfhood" and so on, and interpreted as "self-awareness," "self-confidence" etc. This concept was first expounded by Iqbal in his long didactic poem in the book *Asrar Khudi* (Secrets of the Self), which he wrote in 1915, and which was translated by Nicholson, who had previously been his examiner at Cambridge. It is a great honour for a pupil to have his book translated by his professor. Professor Nicholson translated it and introduced Iqbal and his philosophy to Europe in 1920.

The second theme noted in Iqbal's philosophy is that of constant change, evolution, action and movement. He would not tolerate stagnancy, inaction and immobility, even in Heaven.

The third theme evident in his works is the battle between *'ishq* (love) and *'aql* (intellect), wherein the former has been glorified and the latter depicted as a villain.

Iqbal accorded Man a very high position and discussed in detail the role of Man in the scheme of existence. Rejection of imperialism, capitalism, materialism and nationalism are also constant themes in Iqbal's works.

Iqbal is identified with a number of titles, such as *'Allamah* (Scholar Par Excellence), *Sha'ir Mashriq* (Poet of the East), *Mufakkir Islam* (Ideologue of Islam) and *Hakim al-Ummah* (Wise Man of the Ummah). He is considered one of the greatest poets of all time both in Urdu and Persian. He was noted for his in-depth knowledge of Arabic, Persian and European literature.

Apart from the Holy Qur'an and the life of the prophet Muhammad (s) and of many of his Companions, he was profoundly influenced by Jalal al-Din al-Rumi, the legendary Persian poet and Sufi sage of the thirteenth century, and some Western philosophers such as Friedrich Nietzsche, Henri Bergson and Goethe.

His first Urdu book in prose, *'Ilm al-Iqtisad* (Knowledge of Economics), was written in Urdu in 1903. His first poetic work, *Asrar Khudi* (1915), was followed by *Rumuz Bikhudi* (1917). *Payam Mashriq* appeared in 1923, *Zabur Ajam* in 1927, *Javid Nama* in 1932, *Pas Cheh Bayad Kard Ay Aqwam Sharq* in 1936, and *Armughan Hijaz* in 1938. All these books were in Persian. The last one, published posthumously is mainly in Persian: only a small portion comprises Urdu poems and ghazals.

His first book of poetry in Urdu, *Bang Dara* (1924), was followed by *Bal Jibril* in 1935 and *Zarb Kalim* in 1936. A collection of his English lectures and letters titled *The Reconstruction of Religious Thought in Islam* was published by the Oxford Press.

Iqbal was a close and trusted associate of Muhammed Ali Jinnah, the founder of Pakistan.

The Translator
Abdussalam Puthige
(b. 1964)

Abdussalam Puthige, is a journalist, an author, a translator, a speaker, a trainer and a social activist. He graduated in history from ICE, University of Madras, studied law at SDM Law College, Mangalore, and earned his postgraduate diploma in human rights under the Indian Institute of Human Rights, New Delhi.

He is the chief editor of Vartha Bharathi, a Kannada daily newspaper published simultaneously in Bangalore and Mangalore. He is the founder and director of Madhyama Kendra, a Bangalore-based NGO engaged in media-related studies, research and training.

Puthige has authored six books in Kannada and three in English, and has translated over a couple of dozen books mainly from Urdu to Kannada. His recent work, *Kannadadalli Qur'an Anuvada*, his own translation of the entire Qur'an in Kannada with brief notes, is widely acclaimed for its simple, chaste and lucid style. First published in 2012, it has already seen seven editions. Its third edition was published by the Ministry of Islamic Affairs, Dubai, UAE. His internationally acclaimed work *Towards Performing Da'wah* has been published by the International Council for Islamic Information, Leicester, UK.

Puthige studied Urdu, Arabic and Islamic theology under his father Mawlana Muhammad Shafi'i, and studied Persian literature under the late Mawlana Sayyid Muhammad Yunus.

Shikwa
The Complaint

Stanza (1)

كيوں زياں كار بنوں، سُود فراموش رہوں   فكر فرداٰ نہ كروں محو غم دوش رہوں

Kyun Ziyaan Kaar Banun, Sood Faramosh Rahun
Fikr-e-Farda Na Karum, Mahw-e-Ghum-e-Dosh
Rahun

Why should I remain a loser and ignore my interests?
Why should I confine my concerns to the present and
worry not about the future?

نالٓے بلبل كے سنوں اور ہمہ تن گوش رہوں   ہم نوٓائيں بھی كوئی گل ہوں كہ خاموش رہوں

Naale Bulbul Ke Sunoon, Aur Hama Tan Gosh Rahun
Humnawa Main Bhi Koi Gul Hun Ke Khamosh Rahun

Should I be all ears and meekly listen to the
lamentations of the nightingale?
My companion, am I a mere flower that I should
always remain quiet?

جرأت آموز مری تابِ سخن ہے مجھ كو
شكوہ اللہ سے خاكم بدہن ہے مجھ كو

3

Jurrat Aamoz Meri Taab-e-Sakhun Hai Mujh Ko
Shikwa Allah Se Khakam Badahan Hai Mujh Ko

My ability to articulate dares me to speak.
May God forgive me. My grievance is against none but
Allah.

∾ ∾ ∾

Stanza (2)

ہے بجا شیوۂ تسلیم میں مشہور ہیں ہم   قصّۂ درد سناتے ہیں کہ مجبور ہیں ہم

Hai Baja Shewa-e-Tasleem Mein Mashoor Hain Hum
Qissa-e-Dard Sunate Hain Ke Majboor Hain Hum

It is true that we are well known for our trait of being
subservient,
But now left with no other choice, we must narrate
our tale of woes.

سازِ خاموش ہیں، فریاد سے معمور ہیں ہم   نالہ آتا ہے اگر لب پہ تو معذور ہیں ہم

Saaz-e-Khamosh Hain, Faryad Se Maamoor Hain Hum
Nala Ata Hai Agar Lab Pe To Maazoor Hain Hum

Although we are silent, filled we are with a series of
grievances.
We are so helpless that our grievances have reached
our lips.

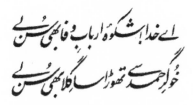

Ae Khuda Shikwa-e-Arbab-e-Wafa Bhi Sun Le
Khugar-e-Hamd Se Thoda Sa Gila Bhi Sun Le

O God, listen to the woes of those who have always
been loyal.
Attend to some grumblings of those who were always
busy praising You.

∾ ∾ ∾

Stanza (3)

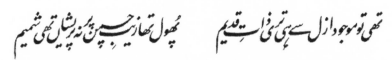

Thi To Maujood Azal Se Hi Teri Zaat-e-Qadim
Phool Tha Zaib-e-Chaman, Par Na Pareshan Thi
Shamim

Although Your eternal being has been perpetually in
existence
Like a flower in the garden, in the absence of any
breeze to deliver its fragrance.

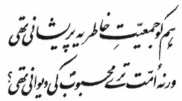

Shart Insaaf Hai, Ae Sahib-e-Altaf-e-Amim
Boo-e-Gul Phailti Kis Tarah Jo Hoti Na Nasim

Is it fair on Your part, then, O absolutely generous
Lord, (not to acknowledge)
That the fragrance of the flower would not reach out
without the help of the flowing wind?

Hum Ko Jamiat-e-Khatir Ye Pareshani Thi
Warna Ummat Tere Mehboob (s) Ki Diwani Thi

Willingly, we took all the pains to perform this task.
Otherwise, do You think the followers of Your
beloved Messenger (s) were insane?

6

Stanza (4)

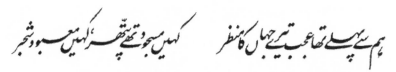

Hum Se Pehle Tha Ajab Tere Jahan Ka Manzar
Kahin Masjood The Pathar, Kahin Maabood Shajar

(God), before our advent, pathetic was the condition
of Your world.
Some prostrated before stones, and others worshipped
trees.

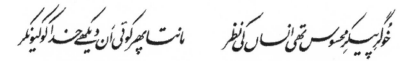

Khugar-e-Paikar-e-Mahsoos Thi Insaan Ki Nazar
Maanta Phir Koi Un-Dekhe Khuda Ko Kyunkar

People were seasoned to see divinity only in objects
tangible.
Least prepared were they to accept the God unseen.

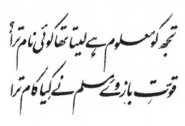

Tujh Ko Maalum Hai Leta Tha Koi Naam Tera?
Quwwat-e-Baazoo-e-Muslim Ne Kiya Kaam Tera

Was there anybody, then, in Your knowledge who
uttered Your name?
It was the might of the Muslims that promoted Your
cause.

ৰ ৰ ৰ

Stanza (5)

بس رہے تھے یہیں سلجوق بھی تُورانی بھی ۔ اہلِ چیں چین میں، ایران میں ساسانی بھی

Bas Rahe The Yahin Saljuq Bhi, Toorani Bhi
Ahl-e-Chin Cheen Mein, Iran Mein Sasaani Bhi

Once dwelled here the Seljuks and the Turanians.
The Chinese were in China, and in Persia were the
Sasanians.

اسی معمورے میں آباد تھے یونانی بھی ۔ اسی دنیا میں یہودی بھی تھے، نصرانی بھی

Issi Maamoore Mein Aabad The Yoonani Bhi
Issi Dunya Mein Yahudi Bhi The, Nusraani Bhi

Greeks lived too in this habitat,
And so did the communities of Jews and Christians.

8

پر تیرے نام پہ تلوار اُٹھائی کس نے

بات جو بگڑی ہوئی تھی، وہ بنائی کس نے

Par Tere Naam Pe Talwar Utai Kis Ne
Baat Jo Bigdi Huwi Thi, Woh Banaai Kis Ne

But who was it that raised the sword in Your name?
Who was it that set right everything that had gone
wrong?

ॐ ॐ ॐ

Stanza (6)

تھے ہمیں ایک تیرے معرکہ آراؤں میں خشکیوں میں کبھی لڑتے، کبھی دریاؤں میں

The Hameen Ek Therey Maarka Aaraaon Mein!
Khushkion Mein Kabhi Ladte, Kabhi Dariyaon Mein,

None else but us were the warriors who fought
Battles for Your sake in the lands and in the seas.

دیں اذانیں کبھی یورپ کے کلیساؤں میں کبھی افریقہ کے تپتے ہوئے صحراؤں میں

Dee Azaanen Kabhi Europe Ke Kaleesaaon Mein
Kabhi Africa Ke Tapte Huwe Sehraaon Mein.

We at times proclaimed the *adhan* in the churches of
Europe
And on the burning sands of the African deserts.

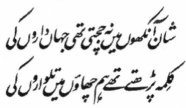

Shan Ankhon Mein Na Jachti Thi Jahan Daron Ki
Kalima Padte The Hum Chaon Mein Talwaron Ki

Luxuries of the rich monarchs never lured us.
We pronounced the *kalimah* under the shadow of the
swords.

∽ ∽ ∽

Stanza (7)

Hum Jo Jeete The To Jangon Ki Musibat Ke Liye
Aur Marte The Tere Naam Ki Azmat Ke Liye

We lived only to suffer the perils of war,
And we offered our lives to advance the glory of Your
name.

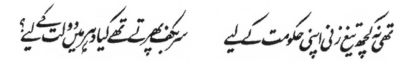

Thi Na Kuch Thaeg-Zani Apni Hukumat Ke Liye
Sar-Bakaf Phirte The Kya Dehar Mein Doulat Ke Liye

It never was for the sake of power that we took up
swords.
Do You think we risked our lives for the sake of mere
treasures?

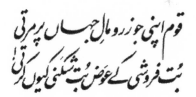

Qaum Apni Jo Zar-o-Maal-e-Jahan Par Marti,
Buth Faroshi Ke Iwaz Buth Shikani Kyon Karti?

If wealth were the real motto behind our missions,
Why would we resort to smashing the idols and not
sell them instead?

11

Stanza (8)

مٹ نہ سکتے تھے اگر جنگ میں اڑ جاتے تھے ۔ ۔ ۔ پاؤں شیروں کے بھی میداں سے اکھڑ جاتے تھے

Tal Na Sakte The Agar Jang Mein Adh Jate The
Paon Sheron Ke Bhi Maidan Se Ukhad Jate The

Once in the battle front, we were firm like rocks.
We made even the bravest of our opponents quiver in
the field.

تجھ سے سرکش ہوا کوئی تو بگڑ جاتے تھے ۔ ۔ ۔ تیغ کیا چیز ہے ہم توپ سے لڑ جاتے تھے

Tujh Se Sarkash Huwa Koi Tho Bighad Jate The
Thaeg Kya Cheez Hai, Hum Thop Se Ladh Jathe The

Any sign of rebellion against You would agitate us.
Let alone the swords, we confronted the cannons too.

نقش توحید کا ہر دل پہ بٹھایا ہم نے
زیر خنجر بھی یہ پیغام سنایا ہم نے

Naqsh Tauheed Ka Har Dil Pe Bithaya Hum Ne
Zer-e-Khanjar Bhi Yeh Paigham Sunaya Hum Ne

We inscribed in every heart, faith in Your oneness.
While facing the swords of the foes, too, we conveyed
Your word.

∼ ∼ ∼

Stanza (9)

تُو ہی کہہ دے کہ اکھاڑا درِ خیبر کس نے شہر قیصر کا جو تھا، اُس کو کیا سر کس نے

Thu Hi Keh De Ke Ukhada Dar-e-Khyber Kis Ne
Sheher Qaiser Ka Jo Tha, Us Ko Kiya Sar Kis Ne

Tell us who wrecked the gate of Khaybar?
Who conquered the city that once belonged to Caesar?

توڑے مخلوق خداوندوں کے پیکر کس نے کاٹ کر رکھ دیے کُفّار کے لشکر کس نے

Thore Makhluq Khudawandon Ke Paikar Kis Ne
Kaat Kar Rakh Diye Kuffaar Ke Lashkar Kis Ne

Who destroyed the creations that were attributed to
divinity?
Who crushed the mighty forces of the infidels?

13

کس نے ٹھنڈا کیا آتش کدۂ ایران کو؟
کس نے پھر زندہ کیا تذکرۂ یزداں کو؟

Kis Ne Thanda Kiya Atishkuda-e-Iran Ko?
Kis Ne Phir Zinda Kiya Tazkara-e-Yazdaan Ko?

Who doused the fiery urns of Iran?
Who revived the glory of Yazdan?

෴ ෴ ෴

Stanza (10)

کون سی قوم فقط تیری طلب گار ہوئی   اور تیرے لیے زحمت کش پیکار ہوئی

Kon Si Qoum Faqat Teri Talabgaar Huwi
Aur Tere Liye Zehmat Kash-e-Paikaar Huwi

Which was the nation that sought none but You
And took all the toils only for Your sake?

کس کی شمشیر جہاں گیر جہاں دار ہوئی   کس کی تکبیر سے دنیا تری بیدار ہوئی

Kis Ki Shamsheer Jahangeer, Jahandar Huwi
Kis Ki Takbeer Se Dunya Teri Baidar Huwi

14

Whose blade was it that conquered and governed the
world?
Whose *takbir* was it that awakened Your world?

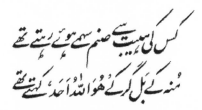

Kis Ki Haibat Se Sanam Sehme Huwe Rehte The
Munh Ke Bal Gir Ke 'HU WA-ALLAH HU AHAD'
Kehte The

Who was it that the idols were in horror of?
Who caused them to kiss the dust and cry, "*Hu Allah*
ahad" (He is Allah, one)?

๛ ๛ ๛

Stanza (11)

Aa Gaya Ain Ladaai Mein Agar Waqt-e-Namaz
Qibla Ru Ho Ke Zameen Bos Huwi Qoum-e-Hijaz

While even in the midst of war, when it was time for
prayer,
This community of Hijaz fell in prostration, facing the
prescribed direction.

Ek Hi Saf Mein Khade Ho Gaye Mahmood-o-Ayaz,
No Koi Banda Raha Aur Na Koi Banda Nawaz.

Kings and slaves stood in the same line.
No discrimination remained between the master and
the slave.

Banda-o-Sahib-o-Mauhtaaj-o-Ghani Aik Huwe
Teri Sarkar Mein Pohanche To Sabhi Aik Huwe

The slave and the master, the wretched and the
affluent, merged.
All were one when they reached Your divine court.

16

Stanza (12)

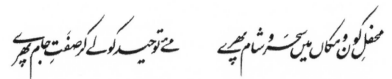

Mehfil-e-Kon-o-Makan Mein Sehar-o-Sham Phire
Mai-e-Tauheed Ko Lekar Sifat-e-Jam Phire

Day and night, we roamed around this world of time
and space,
Carrying the wine of Your message of unity like a mug
in rotation.

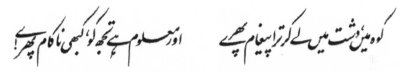

Koh Mein, Dasht Mein Le Kar Tera Paigham Phire
Aur Maaloom Hai Tujh Ko, Kabhi Nakaam Phire!

We wandered over the lands and the seas, propagating
Your message.
Did You ever see us fail in any of our missions?

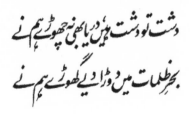

Dasht To Dasht Hain, Darya Bhi Na Chhode Hum Ne
Bahr-e-Zulmaat Mein Dauda Diye Ghode Hum Ne

Let alone the land, we did not spare the seas either.
We rode our horses through the dark seas too.

᭠ ᭠ ᭠

Stanza (13)

صفحۂ دہر سے باطل کو مٹایا ہم نے نوعِ انساں کو غلامی سے چھڑایا ہم نے

Safah-e-Dahar Se Baatil Ko Mitaya Hum Ne
Nau-e-Insaan Ko Ghulami Se Chhudaya Hum Ne

We erased falsehood from the surface of the earth.
We liberated the enslaved mankind from slavery.

تیرے کعبے کو جبینوں سے بسایا ہم نے تیرے قرآن کو سینوں سے لگایا ہم نے

Tere Kaabe Ko Jabeenon Se Basaya Hum Ne
Tere Quran Ko Seenon Se Lagaya Hum Ne

We beautified Your Ka'bah with our foreheads bowed.
We held Your Qur'an to our hearts.

پھر بھی ہم سے یہ گلہ ہے کہ وفادار نہیں

ہم وفادار نہیں، تُو بھی تو دلدار نہیں!

Phir Bhi Hum Se Yeh Gila Hai Ke Wafadar Nahin
Hum Wafadar Nahin, Tu Bhi To Dildar Nahin!

And now You accuse us of not being loyal?
If we are not loyal, You too have not been generous
enough.

∾ ∾ ∾

Stanza (14)

اُمتیں اور بھی ہیں اُن میں گنہگار بھی ہیں   عجز والے بھی ہیں مستِ مے پندار بھی ہیں

Ummatain Aur Bhi Hain, In Mein Gunahgar Bhi Hain
Ejz Wale Bhi Hain, Mast-e-Mai-e-Pindar Bhi Hain

There are many communities out there and among
them are sinners too.
Some of them are humble and some are arrogant too.

ان میں کاہل بھی ہیں غافل بھی ہیں ہشیار بھی ہیں   سیکڑوں ہیں کہ تیرے نام سے بیزار بھی ہیں

In Mein Kaahil Bhi Hain, Ghaafil Bhi Hain, Hoshyar
Bhi Hain
Saikdon Hain Ke Tere Naam Se Baizar Bhi Hain

Some among them are lethargic, some unaware and a
few brilliant too.
There are hundreds of them who are averse even to
Your name.

رحمتیں ہیں تری اغیار کے کاشانوں پر

برق گرتی ہے تو بیچارے مسلمانوں پر

Rehmatain Hain Teri Aghiyar Ke Kashaanon Par
Barq Girti Hai Tho Bechare Musalmanon Par

But You have been showering Your blessings on the
castes of the hostile,
And Your rage always befalls the helpless Muslims.

ن ن ن

Stanza (15)

بت صنم خانوں میں کہتے ہیں مسلمان گئے   ہے خوشی ان کو کہ کعبے کے نگہبان گئے

20

Buth Sanam Khanon Mein Kehte Hain, Musalman Gaye
Hai Khushi In Ko Ke Kaabe Ke Nigehban Gaye

Idols in the temples are rejoicing that Muslims are gone.
They are in delight that the guardians of the Ka'bah are gone.

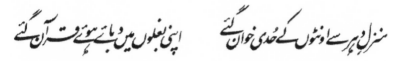

Manzil-e-dehr Se Unthon Ke Hudi Khawan Gaye
Apni Baghlon Mein Dabaye Huwe Quran Gaye

Those singing camel riders have vanished from the surface of the earth.
They have left for ever, with their Qur'ans folded under their arms.

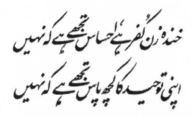

Khandah Zan Kufr Hai, Ehsas Tujhe Hai Ke Nahin
Apni Touheed Ka Kuch Paas Tujhe Hai Ke Nahin

Are You aware at all that the infidels are in great joy?
Do You have any amount of concern for the message
of Your oneness?

ෲ ෲ ෲ

Stanza (16)

یہ شکایت نہیں ہیں اُن کے خزانے معمور نہیں محفل میں جنہیں بات بھی کرنے کا شعور

Ye Shikayatt Nahin, Hain Un Ke Khazane Maamur
Nahin Mehfil Mein Jinhain Baat Bhi Karne Ka Shaur

Let us say without any malice that such are in
affluence today
Who lack the skills even to speak in a decent
convention.

قہر تو یہ ہے کہ کافر کو ملیں حور و قصور اور بیچارے سلماں کو فقط وعدۂ حور

Qehar To Ye Hai Ke Kafir Ko Milain Hoor-o-Qasoor
Aur Bechare Musalman Ko Faqat Wada-e-Hoor

It is a tragedy indeed that infidels are granted virgins
and castles
While the poor Muslims are left with mere promises
of virgins in Heaven.

22

اب وہ الطاف نہیں ہم پہ عنایات نہیں

بات یہ کیا ہے کہ پہلی سی مدارات نہیں

Ab Woh Altaf Nahin, Hum Pe Anayat Nahin
Baat Ye Kya Hai Ke Pehli Si Madarat Nahin

Today You are no longer kind to us or generous.
Why is it that the warmth of Yours is now a matter of
the past?

൞ ൞ ൞

Stanza (17)

کیوں مسلمانوں میں ہے دولتِ دنیا نایاب   تیری قدرت تو ہے وہ جس کی نہ حد ہے نہ حساب

Kyun Musalmanon Mein Hai Doulat-e-Dunya Nayaab
Teri Qudrat Tho Hai Woh Jis Ki Na Had Hai Na Hisab

Why are Muslims deprived of the fortunes of this
world
When Your might has neither limits nor bounds?

تو جو چاہے تو اُٹھے سینہ صحرا سے حباب   رہرووِ دشت ہے سیلیٰ اُدہ موجِ سراب

Thu Jo Chahe Tho Ute Seena-e-Sehra Se Habab
Rahroo-e-Dasht Ho Seeli Zada Mouj-e-Saraab

Fountains will gush forth from the deserts if You so
wish,
And so can You cause not mirages but rivers to flow
for the voyager on the sands.

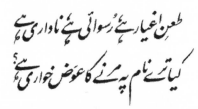

Taan-e-Aghiyaar Hai, Ruswai Hai, Nadaari Hai,
Kya Tere Nam Pe Marne Ka Iwaz Khwari Hai?

Today we are in the midst of hostile taunts,
humiliation and destitution.
Is this how You reward us for sacrificing our lives for
the glory of Your name?

∾ ∾ ∾

Stanza (18)

Bani Aghyar Ki Ab Chahne Wali Dunya

24

Reh Gayi Apne Liye Aik Khayali Dunya

Today the world is fond of the strangers,
And we are left in a world of mere fantasies.

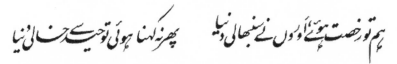

Hum To Rukhsat Huwe, Auron Ne Sanbhali Dunya
Phir Na Kehna Huwi Touheed Se Khali Dunya

As we have left and others have taken charge of the
affairs of this world,
Blame us not that the world is deprived of faith in
Your unity.

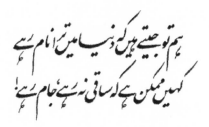

Hum Tho Jeete Hain Ke Duniya Mein Thera Naam
Rahe,
Kahin Mumkin Hai Saqi Na Rahe, Jaam Rahe?

We just lived to make that Your glory remains in the
world.

Is it ever possible for the wine to remain after the cupbearer has left?

∾ ∾ ∾

Stanza (19)

تیری محفل بھی گئی، چاہنے والے بھی گئے،   شب کی آہیں بھی گئیں، صبح کے نالے بھی گئے

Teri Mehfil Bhi Gaye, Chahne Wale Bhi Gaye,
Shab Ki Aahen Bhi Gaye, Subah Ke Nale Bhi Gaye,

Your court is now deserted and Your fans have all left.
No longer are heard those sighs of the midnight and
those prayers of the wee hours.

دل تجھے دے بھی گئے، اپنا صلہ لے بھی گئے،   آ کے بیٹھے بھی نہ تھے اور نکالے بھی گئے

Dil Tujhe Dey bhi Gaye, Apna Sila Le Bhi Gaye,
Aa Ke Baithe Bhi Na The, Ke Nikaale Bhi Gaye.

We offered You our hearts and we took our reward.
We were hardly seated in Your court and were shown
the doors.

26

آئے عشاق، گئے وعدہ فردا لے کر

اب اُنھیں ڈھونڈ چراغِ رُخِ زیبا لے کر

Aaye Ushaaq, Gaye Waada-e-Farda Lekar,
Ab Unhen Dhoond Charag-e-Rukh-e-Zeba Lekar!

Your lovers who came to You are left with a mere
promise of a glorious future.
Now You go in search of them with the light of Your
glowing face.

൮ ൮ ൮

Stanza (20)

دردِ لیلیٰ بھی وہی، قیس کا پہلو بھی وہی   نجد کے دشت و جبل میں رمِ آہو بھی وہی

Dard-e-Laila Bhi Wohi, Qais Ka Pahlu Bhi Wohi,
Nejd Ke Dasht-o-Jabal Mein Ram-e-Aahoo Bhi Wohi,

The agony of Layla is the same and so is the pain of
Qays (Majnun).
In the plains and hills of Najd are seen the same herds
of leaping gazelles.

27

Ishq Ka Dil Bhi Wohi, Husn Ka Jaadoo Bhi Wohi,
Ummat-e-Ahmed-e-Mursil Bhi Wohi, Tu Bhi Wohi,

The spirit of love is the same. The magic of beauty is
the same as well.
Same is the community of Muhammad the Apostle
(s), and so are You.

Phir Yeh Aazurdagi-e-Ghair-Sabab Kya Maani,
Apne Shaidaaon Pe Yeh Chashm-e-Ghazab Kya Maani?

Then what justifies this unfounded estrangement of
Yours?
Why are You looking at Your own devotees with such
rage?

ॐ ॐ ॐ

Stanza (21)

Tujh Ko Choda Ke Rasool-e-Arabi (s) Ko Choda?
Bhuthgari Pesha Kiya, Bhut Shikani Ko Choda?

Did we ever desert You or Your Arabian Messenger (s)?
Did we choose to trade idols? Or did we give up the tradition of smashing them?

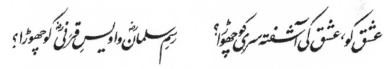

Ishq Ko, Ishq Ki Ashuftah-Sari Ko Choda?
Rasm-e-Salman (r.a.)-o-Awais-e-Qarani (r.a.) Ko Choda?

Did we forsake our love – our insane love – for You?
Or did we stray away from the path of Salman (al-Farisi) (r) and Uways al-Qarani (r).

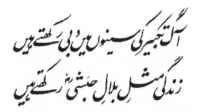

Aag Takbeer Ki Seenon Mein Dabi Rakhte Hain
Zindagi Misl-e-Bilal-e-Habshi (r.a.) Rakhte Hain

29

The same old flames of *takbir* remain hidden in our bosoms.
We live our lives in the same manner as did Bilal the Abyssinian.

∾ ∾ ∾

Stanza (22)

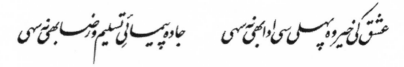

Ishq Ki Khair, Who Pehli Si Ada Bhi Na Sahi,
Jaada Paimaa Taslim-o-Raza Bhi Na Sahi,

It is true that our love today is not of the same calibre as it was in the past
And we are no longer as loyal and obedient as we used to be.

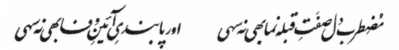

Muztarib Dil Sifat-e-Qibla Numa Bhi Na Sahi
Aur Pabandi-e-Aaeen-e-Wafa Bhi Na Sahi

No longer do we have the heart that was as restless as the needle of the compass,

And we admit we failed in abiding by the rules of
submission and loyalty.

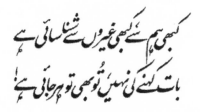

Kabhi Hum Se, Kabhi Ghairon Se Shanasaai Hai
Baat Kehne Ki Nahin, Tu Bhi To Harjaai Hai

But You were with us sometimes and with strangers
sometimes.
Sadly, though, we must say You too have not been
very consistent in Your affection.

ঙ ঙ ঙ

Stanza (23)

Sar-e-Faran Pe Kiya Deen Ko Kamil Tu Ne
Ek Ishare Mein Hazaron Ke Liye Dil Tu Ne

You perfected Your religion on the peak of Mount
Faran (Makkah).

By one gesture of Yours, You won thousands of hearts.

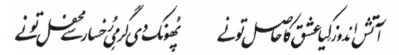

Atish Andoz Kiya Ishq Ka Hasil Tu Ne
Phoonk Di Garmi-e-Rukhsar Se Mehfil Tu Ne

But You set on fire all the fruits of our love,
Then You burnt down the entire assembly with the warm blow of Your cheeks.

Aaj Kyun Seene Humare Sharar Abad Nahin
Hum Wohi Sokhta Saman Hain, Tujhe Yaad Nahin?

Why no fire is found in our bosoms today?
We were the ones that had burnt down all that we had.
Don't You remember?

Stanza (24)

واد یِ نجد میں وہ شورِ سلاسل نہ رہا   قیس دیوانۂ نظارۂ محمل نہ رہا

Wadi-e-Najd Mein Woh Shor-e-Silasil Na Raha
Qais Diwana-e-Nazara Mehmil Na Raha

Today in the valley of Najd those endless sounds of
chains are no longer being heard.
Qays is no longer eager to see who is on the saddle of
the camel.

حوصلے وہ نہ رہے ہم نہ رہے دل نہ رہا   گھر یہ اُجڑا ہے کہ تو رونقِ محفل نہ رہا

Hosle Woh Na Rahe, Hum Na Rahe, Dil Na Raha
Ghar Ye Ujhda Hai Ke Thu Ronaq-e-Mehfil Na Raha

The valour of those days is gone. Gone are we and so
are our hearts.
This house stands ruined because You are no longer in
the house to brighten it.

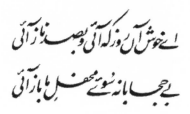

Ae Khush Aan Roz Ke Ayi-o-Basad Naz Ayi
Be-Hijabana Soo'ay Mehfil-e-Ma Baaz Ayi

Oh that glorious day when You will come with great
grandeur.
You will come back to us without hiding Yourself
behind any veil.

∽ ∽ ∽

Stanza (25)

باده کش غیر ہیں گلشن میں لب جو بیٹھے   سُنتے ہیں جام بکف نغمہ کوکو بیٹھے

Badahkash Gair Hain Gulshan Mein Lab-e-Joo Baite
Sunthe Hain Jaam Bakaf Naghma-e-Kuku Baite

Those in the garden today, with their lips sticking to
the wine glass, are aliens.
They are busy holding their wine pots and listening to
the whistles of the cuckoos.

دور ہنگامہ گلزار سے یک سو بیٹھے   تیرے دیوانے بھی ہیں منتظر ہو بیٹھے

Door Hungama-e-Gulzar Se Yak Soo Baite
Tere Diwane Bhi Hain Muntazir 'Hoo' Baite

34

Sitting in a corner, far away from the tumult of the
garden,
Are Your fans in wait of the cry of *Hu* (He).

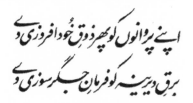

Apne Parwanon Ko Phir Zauq-e-Khud Afrozi De
Barq-e-Dairina Ko Farman-e-Jigar Sozi De

Grant once again the passion of self immolation to the
flies circling around Your flames.
Command that age old lightning to strike and
brighten the hearts.

∾ ∾ ∾

Stanza (26)

Qoum-e-Awara Anaa Taab Hai Phir Soo'ay Hijaz
Le Uda Bulbul-e-Be Par Ko Mazak-e-Parwaz

The wandering community has started marching
towards Hijaz, holding the bridle strings.

The resolve to fly has enabled even the nightingale without wings to fly high.

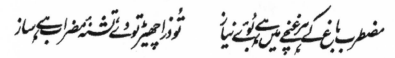

Muztarib Bagh Ke Har Ghunche Mein Hai Boo'ay Niaz
Tu Zara Chahir To De, Tashna-e-Mizrab Hai Saaz

Every branch of the garden is filled with the fragrance of obedience.
You just touch the strings and music is longing to come to life through the plectrum.

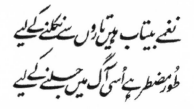

Naghme Betaab Hain Taron Se Niklne Ke Liye
Toor Muztar Hai Ussi Aag Mein Jalne Ke Liye

The melody is restless, longing to spring out of the strings.
Mount Sinai is once again willing to get burnt in the same old fire.

Stanza (27)

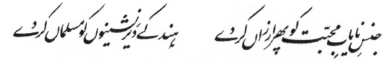

Mushkilain Ummat-e-Marhoom Ki Asan Kar De
Moor-e-Bemaya Ko Humdosh-e-Suleman Kar De

(Our Lord,) make things easy for Your chosen community.
Make the unworthy ants the companions of Sulayman.[1]

Jins-e-Nayaab-e-Mohabbat Ko Phir Arzaan Kar De
Hind Ke Dair Nasheenon Ko Musalman Kar De

Today, love is an absent species. Make it available in abundance.
Bring into the fold of Islam the dwellers of Indian temples.

---

1. Ref / Qur'an 27: 17 to 19.

جوۓ خوں می چکد از حسرتِ دیرینۂ ما

می تپد ناله بہ نشترکدۂ سینۂ ما

Joo'ay Khoon Mee Chakad Az Hasrat-e-Dairina-e-Maa
Mee Tapad Nala Ba Nashtar Kadah-e-Seena-e-Maa

Our long-cherished desires that remain unfulfilled
have drained our blood.
Our hearts pierced so often are in deep pain and agony.

❧ ❧ ❧

Stanza (28)

بوۓ گل لے گئی بیرونِ چمن راز چمن   کیا قیامت ہے کہ خود پھول ہیں غمازِ چمن !

Boo-e-Gul Le Gayi Bairun-e-Chaman Raaz-e-Chaman
Kya Qayamat Hai Ke Khud Phool Hain Ghammaz-e-
Chaman !

The fragrance of the flower has revealed the secrets of
the garden to the world outside.
What a tragedy! None else but the flowers have turned
to be spies against the garden.

عہدِ گل ختم ہوا ٹوٹ گیا سازِ چمن ۔۔۔۔ اُڑ گئے ڈالیوں سے زمزمہ پردازِ چمن

Ahd-e-Gul Khatam Hua, Toot Gaya Saaz-e-Chaman,
Ud Gaye Dalion Se Zamzama Pardaaz-e-Chaman.

The era of the flowers is gone, and gone is the glory of
the garden.
The flying and singing birds have abandoned the
branches of the trees.

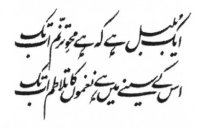

Ek Bulbul Hai Ke Hai Mahw-e-Tarannum Ab Tak,
Us Ke Seene Mein Hai Naghmon Ka Talatam Ab Tak.

But one lone bulbul remains busy singing till this day.
Waves of melody are rising in his heart till this day.

ꙮ ꙮ ꙮ

Stanza (29)

قمریاں شاخِ صنوبر سے گریزاں بھی ہوئیں ۔۔۔۔ پتیاں پھول کی جھڑ جھڑ کے پریشاں بھی ہوئیں

Qumrian Shaakh-e-Sanober Se Gurezaan Bhi Huin,
Pattian Phool Ki Jhar Jhar Ke Pareshan Bhi Huin;

Doves have fled from the branches of the pine trees.
The petals of the flowers have all fallen and lie
scattered.

ڈالیاں پیرہنِ برگ سے اُڑیاں بھی ہوئیں   وہ پُرانی روشیں باغ کی ویراں بھی ہوئیں

Who Purani Ravishen Bagh Ki Weeran Bhi Huin,
Daalian Pairahan-e-Barg Se Udiaan Bhi Huin.

Gardens are desolate and have lost their old looks.
Without leaves to cover them, branches appear
undressed.

قیدِ موسم سے طبیعت رہی آزاد اس کی
کاش گلشن میں سمجھتا کوئی فریاد اس کی!

Qaid-e-Mausim Se Tabiat Rahi Aazad Uski,
Kaash Gulshan Mein Samjhta Koi Faryaad Uski.

He, however, is free from the bonds of the seasons.
Alas! Would somebody in the garden appreciate his
wail?

40

Stanza (30)

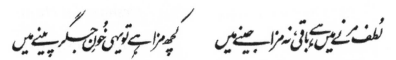

Lutf Marne Main Hai Baqi, Na Maza Jeene Mein
Kuch Maza Hai Tho Yehi Khoon-e-Jigar Peene Mein

There is no pleasure left in death and no fun
remaining in life.

If any joy is left at all, it is only in sipping the blood of
the heart.

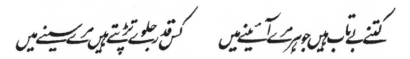

Kitne Betaab Hain Jouhar Mere Aaeene Mein
Kis Qadar Jalwe Tadapte Hain Mere Seene Mein

Many are the hidden gems restless in my bosom.
Many are the visions waiting to unfold within my heart.

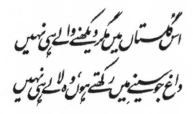

Iss Gulistan Mein Magar Dekhne Wale Hi Nahin
Dagh Jo Seene Mein Rakhte Hon, Woh Lale Hi Nahin

No longer is found any spectator in the garden.
There is no tulip around that holds pain in its heart.

∾ ∾ ∾

Stanza (31)

چاک اس بلبلِ تنہا کی نوا سے دل ہوں جاگنے والے اسی بانگِ درا سے دل ہوں

Chaak Iss Bulbul-e-Tanha Ki Nawa Se Dil Hon
Jaagne Wale Issi Bang-e-Dara Se Dil Hon

May the hearts get split apart with the wailing of the
lonely bulbul.
May the hearts wake up at this marching call.

یعنی پھر زندہ نئے عہدِ وفا سے دل ہوں پھر اسی بادۂ دیرینہ کے پیاسے دل ہوں

Yani Phir Zinda Naye Ehd-e-Wafa Se Dil Hon
Phir Issi Bada-e-Deerina Ke Pyaase Dil Hon

May the renewed spirit of loyalty enliven the hearts
again.
May the hearts feel the thirst once again for the same
old wine.

عجمی خُوں ہے تو کیا ہے تو حجازی ہے مری

نغمہ ہندی ہے تو کیا ہے تو حجازی ہے مری

Ajami Khoon Hai Tho Kya, Mai Tho Hijazi Hai Meri
Naghma Hindi Hai Tho Kya, Lai Tho Hijazi Hai Meri

Never mind the *ʿajami* (non-Arab) blend – my wine is
Hijazi (Arabian) after all.
Never mind that my song is Indian – my melody is
Hijazi after all.

Jawab Shikwa
The Answer to the Complaint

Stanza (1)

دل سے جو بات نکلتی ہے اثر رکھتی ہے ۔ پر نہیں طاقتِ پرواز مگر رکھتی ہے

Dil Se Jo Baat Nikalti Hai, Asar Rakhti Hai
Par Nahin, Taaqat-e-Parwaaz Magar Rakhti Hai

Words that spring from the heart make an impact.
Without wings, they still possess the power to fly.

قدسی الاصل ہے رفعت پہ نظر رکھتی ہے ۔ خاک سے اٹھتی ہے گردوں پہ گزر رکھتی ہے

Qudsi-Ul-Asal Hai, Riffat Pe Nazar Rakhti Hai
Khaak Se Ut'thi Hai, Gardoon Pe Guzar Rakhti Hai

They have their roots in the heaven and therefore
aspire to reach great heights.
They rise from the hearts but travel across the skies.

عشق تھا فتنہ گرو سرکش و چالاک مرا
آسماں چیر گیا نالۂ بے باک مرا

Ishq Tha Fitna Gar-o-Sarkash-o-Chalaak Mera
Aasman Cheer Gaya Nala-e-Bebaak Mera

My love was mischievous, rebellious and quite shrewd.

And My bold cry could finally break into space.

~ ~ ~

Stanza (2)

پیر گردوں نے کہا سن کے، کہیں ہے کوئی   بولے سیّارے، سرِ عرشِ بریں ہے کوئی

Peer-e-Gardoon Ne Kaha Sun Ke, Kahin Hai Koi!
Bole Sayyaare, Sar-e-Arsh-e-Bareen Hai Koi!

On hearing the cry, the old sky said, "There is
somebody around."
Planets said, "There is somebody near the divine
throne."

چاند کہتا تھا، نہیں! اہلِ زمیں ہے کوئی   کہکشاں کہتی تھی، پوشیدہ یہیں ہے کوئی

Chaand Kahta Tha, Nahin, Ahl-e-Zameen Hai Koi!
Kehkashaan Kehti Thi, Poshida Yahin Hai Koi!

The moon said, "No, it is somebody from earth."
The galaxy said, "Somebody is hiding somewhere
nearby."

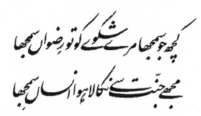

Kuch Jo Samjha Tho Mere Shikwe Ko Rizwan Samjha
Mujhe Jannat Se Nikala Huwa Insan Samjha

It was only Ridwan who understood My complaint to some extent.
He recognised that I was the one driven away from Heaven.[1]

ॐ ॐ ॐ

Stanza (3)

Thi Farishton Ko Bhi Hairat, Ke Yeh Awaz Hai Kya!
Arsh Walon Pe Bhi Khulta Nahin Yeh Raaz Hai Kya!

Angels were wondering whose voice that was.
Those around the divine throne, too, failed to unravel the mystery.

---

1. Ridwan: the custodian of Heaven.

تاسرِعرش بھی انساں کی تگ و تاز ہے کیا؟   آگئی خاک کی چٹکی کو بھی پرواز ہے کیا!

Tha Sar-e-Arsh Bhi Insan Ki Thaeg-o-Taaz Hai Kya?
Aa Gayi Khak Ki Chutki Ko Bhi Parwaaz Hai Kya?

Has the voice of man attained the power to reach the
heavens?
Has that product of clay mastered the art of flying?

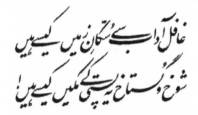

Ghafil Aadaab Se Yeh Sukkaan-e-Zameen Kaise Hain
Shokh-o-Gustakh Yeh Pasti Ke Makeen Kaise Hain!

How ignorant of etiquette these earthly beings are!
How crude the manners of these dwellers of that lowly
region are!

☙ ☙ ☙

Stanza (4)

اس قدر شوخ کہ اللہ سے بھی برہم ہے   تھا جو مسجودِ ملائک یہ وہی آدم ہے؟

Iss Qadar Shokh Ke Allah Se Bhi Barham Hai
Tha Jo Masjood-e-Malaeek Yeh Wohi Aadam Hai?

Is he so arrogant that he is unhappy with Allah?
Is he the same Adam the angels bowed before?

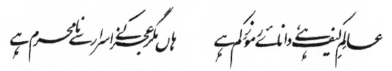

Alam-e-Kaif Hai, Dana-e-Ramooz-e-Kam Hai
Haan, Magar Ijz Ke Asrar Se Namehram Hai

Yes, he knows weights and measures and has
knowledge of some secrets,
But he knows nothing about the hidden virtues of
humility.

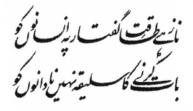

Naaz Hai Taaqat-e-Guftaar Pe Insanon Ko
Baat Karne Ka Saliqa Nahin Nadanon Ko!

Humans are proud that they can articulate,
But the fools do not know the manners of speech.

Stanza (5)

آئی آواز غم انگیز ہے افسانہ ترا   اشک بیتاب سے لبریز ہے پیمانہ ترا

Ayi Aawaz Ghum-Angaiz Hai Afsana Tera
Ashk-e-Betaab Se Labraiz Hai Paimana Tera

Then emerged a voice: Yes, your tale is really sad.
Those gushing tears are too many for your eyes to
contain.

آسماں گیر ہوا نعرہ مستانہ ترا   کس قدر شوخ زباں ہے دل دیوانہ ترا

Asmangeer Huwa Naara-e-Mastana Tera
Kis Qadar Shokh Zuban Hai Dil-e-Diwana Tera

Your passionate cry has occupied the skies.
Oh how bold the speech of your wild heart is!

شکر شکوے کو کیا حسن ادا سے تو نے   ہم سخن کر دیا بندوں کو خدا سے تو نے

Shukr Shikwe Ko Kiya Husn-e-Ada Se Tu Ne
Hum Sukhan Kar Diya Bandon Ko Khuda Se Tu Ne

52

Through your fine articulation you disguised your
complaint as a compliment.
You lead the subjects to converse with their Lord.

ༀ ༀ ༀ

Stanza (6)

راہ دکھلائیں کسے رہرو منزل ہی نہیں   ہم تو مائل بہ کرم ہیں کوئی سائل ہی نہیں

Hum Tho Mayal Ba-Karam Hain, Koi Sayal Hi Nahin
Rah Dikhlaen Kise Rahraw-e-Manzil Hi Nahin

In fact We are always inclined to grant Our mercy, but
there are no seekers.
To whom should we show the path when there is
nobody willing to march towards the destination?

جس سے تعمیر ہو آدم کی یہ وہ گل ہی نہیں   تربیت عام تو ہے جوہر قابل ہی نہیں

Tarbiat Aam Tho Hai, Jauhar-e-Qabil Hi Nahin
Jis Se Taamir Ho Aadam Ki Yeh Woh Gil Hi Nahin

My nourishment is available for all, but there is
nobody deserving it.

That clay from which man could be shaped is available nowhere.

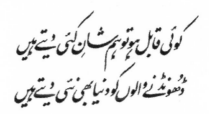

Koi Qabil Ho Tho Hum Shan-e-Kaee Dete Hain
Dhoondne Walon Ko Dunya Bhi Naee Dete Hain!

To those who have merit, We are longing to grant glories.
To those who go exploring, We offer many new worlds.

∾ ∾ ∾

Stanza (7)

Hath Be-Zor Hain, Ilhaad Se Dil Khoo-Gar Hain
Ummati Baais-e-Ruswai-e-Paighamber (s) Hain

Their hands are feeble and hearts are hardened in deviation.

The community of the Prophet (s) is causing him
disgrace.

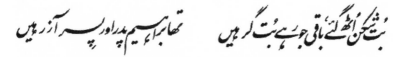

Buth-Shikan Uth Gaye, Baqi Jo Rahe Buth-Gar Hain
Tha Braheem Pidar, Aur Pisar Aazar Hain

Idol breakers having gone, now remain only the idol
worshipers.
Ibrahim (a.s) was their father, but the sons have
become like Azar.[2]

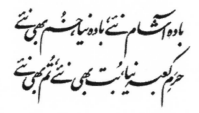

Badah Aasham Naye, Bada Naya, Khum Bhi Naye
Harm-e-Kaaba Naya, Buth Bhi Naye, Thum Bhi Naye

New are the wine consumers, new is the wine and the
flavour is new too.
The Ka'bah is new, idols are new and you are new too.

---

2. Father of Ibrahim (a.s).

Stanza (8)

وہ بھی دن تھے کہ یہی مایہ زیبائی تھا   نازش موسم گل لالہ صحرائی تھا

Woh Bhi Din The Ke Yehi Maya-e-Raanai Tha
Nazish-e-Mousam-e-Gul Lala-e-Sahrai Tha!

There was a time when this was considered the
essence of love.
The tulip of the wild was the hallmark of the spring.

جو مسلمان تھا اللہ کا سودائی تھا   کبھی محبوب تمھارا یہی حرجائی تھا

Jo Musalmaan Tha Allah Ka Saudai Tha
Kabhi Mehboob Tumhara Yehi Harjai Tha

Every Muslim was once a great devotee of Allah,
The one accused of betrayal (God) was once the most
beloved of yours.

کسی یکجائی سے اب عہد غلامی کر لو
ملت احمد مرسل کو مقامی کر لو

Kisi Yakjai Se Ab Ehd-e-Ghulami Kar Lo
Millat-e-Ahmad (s) Ko Maqami Kar Lo!

Now find some loyal God to be your master and make
a covenant of servitude.
Confine the community of Muhammad the
Messenger (s) to some small region.

∾ ∾ ∾

Stanza (9)

Kis Qadar Tum Pe Giran Subah Ki Baidari Hai
Hum Se Kab Pyar Hai! Haan Neend Tumhain Pyari
Hai

How difficult it is for you to wake up early in the
morning!
False is your claim of love for Me. It is in fact your
sleep that you have fallen in love with.

Tabaa-e-Azad Pe Qaid-e-Ramazan Bhari Hai
Tumhi Keh Do, Yehi Aaeen-e-Wafadari Hai?

Love for freedom has made the restrictions of
Ramadan difficult for you.
Tell me, is this the way to prove your loyalty?

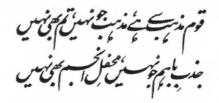

*Qoum Mazhab Se Hai, Mazhab Jo Nahin, Tum Bhi
Nahin*

Jazb-e-Baham Jo Nahin, Mehfil-e-Anjum Bhi Nahin

Faith is the foundation of a nation. Without faith, you
do not exist.
It is like gravitation, without which the union of stars
will cease to exist.

ॐ ॐ ॐ

Stanza (10)

Jin Ko Ata Nahin Dunya Mein Koi Fann, Tum Ho
Nahin Jis Qoum Ko Parwaye Nasheman, Tum Ho

You are the only people in the world ignorant of any skill.
Yours is the only community that is least bothered about its home.

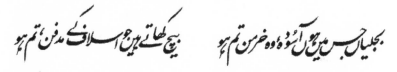

Bijliyan Jis Mein Hon Aasudah, Woh Khirman Tum Ho
Baich Khate Hain Jo Aslaaf Ke Madfan, Tum Ho

Yours is the nest where the lightening finds a place to rest.
You are the people who sell the shroud of their ancestors.

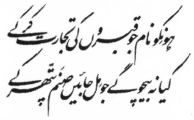

Ho Niko Naam Jo Qabaron Ki Tajarat Kar Ke
Kya Na Baicho Ge Jo Mil Jaen Sanam Pathar Ke

You have earned a reputation for marketing the graves.
Will you hesitate to sell idols if you get some?

∞ ∞ ∞

Stanza (11)

صفحہ دہر سے باطل کو مٹایا کس نے؟ نوعِ انساں کو غلامی سے چھڑایا کس نے؟

Safah-e-Dehr Se Batil Ko Mitaya Kis Ne?
Nau-e-Insan Ko Ghulami Se Chhudaya Kis Ne?

Who erased falsehood from the surface of this earth?
Who liberated mankind from the shackles of
bondage?

میرے کعبے کو جبینوں سے بسایا کس نے؟ میرے قرآن کو سینوں سے لگایا کس نے؟

Mere Kaabe Ko Jabeenon Se Basaya Kis Ne?
Mere Quran Ko Seenon Se Lagaya Kis Ne?

Who populated My Ka'bah with their bowed heads?
Who held My Qur'an fondly close to their hearts?

تھے تو آبا وہ تمھارے ہی مگر تم کیا ہو؟ ہاتھ پر ہاتھ دھرے منتظرِ فردا ہو!

The Tho Aaba Woh Tumhare Hi, Magar Tum Kya Ho?
Hath Par Hath Dhare Muntazir-e-Farda Ho!

It is true that they were your own ancestors. But what
is your merit?
You are sitting idle, waiting for the dawn to come.

∿ ∿ ∿

Stanza (12)

Kya Kaha? "Bahr-e-Musalman Hai Faqt Wade-e-Hoor
Shikwa Be-Ja Bhi Kare Koi Tho Lazim Hai Shaoor!

Did you say Muslims are granted mere promises of
virgins in Heaven?
There should be some sense, at least, in your unjust
laments.

Adal Hai Fatir-e-Hasti Ka Azal Se Dastoor
Muslim Aaeen Huwa Kafir Tho Mile Hoor-o-Qasoor

Justice has been the rule behind the creation of this
universe.

If infidels become true Muslims, virgins and castles in Heaven will all be theirs.

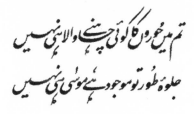

Tum Mein Hooron Ka Koi Chahne Wala Hi Nahin
Jalwa-e-Toor Tau Maujood Hai, Moosa Hi Nahin

In fact among you there is no real seeker of heavenly virgins.
Mount Tur is ready to manifest the divine power, but Musa is nowhere to be found.

∾ ∾ ∾

Stanza (13)

Manfa'at Aik Hai Is Qaum Ki, Nuqsan Bhi Aik
Ek Hi Sab Ka Nabi (s), Din Bhi, Iman Bhi Aik

In matters of your community, loss or gain of one is loss or gain of all.

Your Messenger (s) is one, as is your religion and your faith.

حرَم بھی پاک، اللہ بھی، قرآن بھی ایک   کچھ بڑی بات تھی ہوتے جو مسلمان بھی ایک

Harm-e-Paak Bhi, Allah Bhi, Quran Bhi Aik,
Kuch Badi Baat Thi Hote Jo Musalmaan Bhi Aik!

One is your Ka'bah, one is Allah and one is the Qur'an.
In spite of all this, is the community of Muslims ever seen bound as one?

فرقہ بندی ہے کہیں اور کہیں ذاتیں ہیں
کیا زمانے میں پنپنے کی یہی باتیں ہیں

Firqa Bandi Hai Kahin, Aur Kahin Zaatain Hain
Kya Zamane Mein Panapne Ki Yehi Baatain Hain?

You have divided yourselves into clans and factions.
Is this the how nations flourish in this world?

∾ ∾ ∾

Stanza (14)

كون هے تارکِ آئینِ رسولِ مختار؟ مصلحتِ وقت کی ہے کس کے عمل کا معیار؟

Kon Hai Taarik-e-Aaeen-e-Rasool-e-Mukhtar (s)?
Maslihat Waqt Ki Hai Kis Ke Amal Ka Maayaar?

Who abandoned the code of the Messenger (s)?
Who adopted mere temporal interests as their code of
conduct?

کس کی آنکھوں میں سمایا ہے شعارِ اغیار؟ ہو گئی کس کی نگاہ طرزِ سلف سے بیزار؟

Kis Ki Ankhon Mein Samaya Hai Sha'ar-e-Aghyar
Ho Gayi Kis Ki Nigah Tarz-e-Salaf Se Baizar?

Did you not proudly follow the path of the infidels?
Did you not treat the ways of your own ancestors with
contempt?

قلب میں سوز نہیں، روح میں احساس نہیں
کچھ بھی پیغامِ محمدﷺ کا تمھیں پاس نہیں

Qalb Mein Souz Nahin, Rooh Mein Ehsas Nahin
Kuch Bhi Paigham-e-Muhammad (s) Ka Tumhain
Paas Nahin

64

Your hearts are bereft of passion and your souls have
no zeal.
There is no concern left in you for the message of
Muhammad (s).

∾ ∾ ∾

Stanza (15)

جا کے ہوتے ہیں ساجد میں صف آرا، تو غریب   زحمتِ روزہ جو کرتے ہیں گوارا تو غریب

*Jaa Ke Hote Hain Masajid Mein Saf-Aara, Tho
Ghareeb*
Zehmat-e-Roza Jo Karte Hain Gawara, Tho Ghareeb

Only the poor among you go to the masjid and line up
for prayer.
The hardships of fasting too is reserved for the poor
among you.

نام لیتا ہے اگر کوئی ہمارا، تو غریب   پردہ رکھتا ہے اگر کوئی تمہارا، تو غریب

Naam Leta Hai Agar Koi Hamara, Tau Ghareeb
Pardah Rakhta Hai Agar Koi Tumhara, Tau Ghareeb

It is only the poor who glorify Our name,
And it is the poor who conceal your crime.

اُمرانَشّہِ دولت میں ہیں غافل ہم سے

زندہ ہے مِلّتِ بیضا غُربا کے دم سے

Umra Nasha-e-Doulat Mein Hain Ghafil Hum Se
Zinda Hai Millat-e-Baiza Ghurba Ke Dam Se

The rich are obsessed with their wealth and have
forgotten Us.
It is thanks to the poor that the faith is alive.

ﻌ ﻌ ﻌ

Stanza (16)

واعظِ قوم کی وہ پُختہ خیالی نہ رہی   برق طبعی نہ رہی، شُعلہ مقالی نہ رہی

Waaiz-e-Qoum Ki Woh Pukhta Khayali Na Rahi
Barq Taba'ee Na Rahi, Shaola Maqali Na Rahi

The preachers in your community lack maturity of
thought.
There is no impulse in their personality and no fire in
their words.

رہ گئی رسمِ اذاں رُوحِ بلالی نہ رہی   فلسفہ رہ گیا، تلقینِ غزالی نہ رہی

66

Reh Gayi Rasm-e-Azan, Rooh-e-Bilali Na Rahi
Falsafa Reh Gaya, Talqeen-e-Ghazali Na Rahi

The ritual of *adhan* remains, but the spirit of Bilal is
missing.
Philosophy is found, but not the conviction of
Ghazali.

سجدیں مرثیہ خواں ہیں کہ نمازی نہ رہے

یعنی وہ صاحبِ اوصافِ حجازی نہ رہے

Masjidain Marsiya Khawan Hain Ke Namazi Na Rahe
Yani Woh Sahib-e-Ausaf-e-Hijazi Na Rahe

Masjids are found lamenting that the real devout
worshipers are not visible anywhere,
Meaning those who had Hijazi qualities are found
nowhere.

ᘯ ᘯ ᘯ

Stanza (17)

شورے ہے ہو گئے دنیا سے سلمان نابود   ہم یہ کہتے ہیں کہ تھے بھی کہیں مسلم موجود!

Shor Hai Ho Gaye Dunya Se Musalman Nabood
Hum Ye Kehte Hain Ke The Bhi Kahin Muslim Maujood!

There is a cry all around that Muslims have vanished
from the world.
But let us ask you: Did Muslims really exist anywhere?

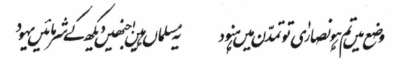

Waza Mein Tum Ho Nisara, Tho Tamaddun Mein
Hanood,
Yeh Musalman Hain! Jinhain Dekh Ke Sharmaen
Yahood?

Your attire is like that of Christians, and in culture
you are Hindus.
You are such Muslims that even Jews will be ashamed
of you.

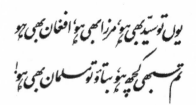

Yun To Syed Bhi Ho, Mirza Bhi Ho, Afghan Bhi Ho
Tum Sabhi Kuch Ho, Batao To Musalman Bhi Ho!

There are Sayyids among you, Mirzas and Afghans too.
But tell us: Is there any Muslim left in your midst?

∾ ∾ ∾

Stanza (18)

دمِ تقریر تھی مسلم کی صداقت بیباک   عدل اس کا تھا قوی، لوثِ مراعات سے پاک

Dam-e-Taqreer Thi Muslim Ki Sadaqat Bebak
Adal Uss Ka Tha Qawi, Loos-e-Mara'at Se Pak

Muslims were known for their honest speech.
They stood strong in justice and were free from greed
for gifts.

شجرِ فطرتِ مسلم تھا حیا سے نمناک   تھا شجاعت میں وہ اک ہستیِ فوق الادراک

Shajar-e-Fitrat-e-Muslim Tha Haya Se Namnak
Tha Shujaat Mein Woh Ek Hasti-e-Fouq-Ul-Idraak

Modesty was an integral part of their character.
In courage and valour they were superhuman.

خود گدازی در نمِ کیفیتِ صہبائش بود
خالی از خویش شدن صورتِ مینائش بود

Khud Gudazi Nam-e-Kaifiat-e-Sehbayesh Bood
Khali Az Khawaish Shudan Soorat-e-Meenayesh Bood

Like wine on the lips, they drained themselves to see
others happy.
Like the cup pouring out the drink, they shed their
lives for the comfort of others.

ℭ ℭ ℭ

Stanza (19)

هر مسلمان رگِ باطل کے لیے نشتر تھا   اُس کے آئینہ ہستی میں عمل جوہر تھا

Har Musalman Rag-e-Batil Ke Liye Nashtar Tha
Uss Ke Aaeena-e-Hasti Mein Amal Jouhar Tha

Every Muslim was a knife on the vein of falsehood.
Noble deeds shone like diamonds in the mirror of his
existence.

جو بھروسہ تھا اُسے قوتِ بازو پر تھا   ہے تمہیں موت کا ڈر اُس کو خدا کا ڈر تھا

Jo Bharosa Tha Usse Quwwat-e-Bazoo Par Tha
Hai Tumhain Mout Ka Dar, Uss Ko Khuda Ka Dar Tha

He had great confidence in his personal strength.
You are scared of death, while he feared none but
God.

باپ کا علم نہ بیٹے کو اگر از بر ہو
پھر پسر قابلِ میراثِ پدر کیونکر ہو!

Baap Ka Ilm Na Bete Ko Agar Azbar Ho
Phir Pisar Qabil-e-Miraas-e-Pidar Kyunkar Ho!

When the son fails to master the skills of his father,
How can he deserve to inherit his father's treasure?

∾ ∾ ∾

Stanza (20)

ہر کوئی مستِ مے ذوقِ تن آسانی ہے   تم مسلماں ہو! یہ اندازِ مسلمانی ہے!

Har Koi Mast-e-Mai-e-Zauq-e-Tan Asani Hai,
Tum Musalman Ho? Ye Andaaz-e-Musalmani Hai?

Each one of you is heavily intoxicated by the wine of
lethargy.

Are you Muslims really? Is such the conduct of Muslims?

حیدری فقر ہے نے دولتِ عثمانی ہے   تم کو اسلاف سے کیا نسبتِ روحانی ہے؟

Haidari Faqr Hai Ne Doulat-e-Usmani Hai
Tum Ko Aslaaf Se Kya Nisbat-e-Rohani Hai?

You have neither the penury of Haydar ('Ali (*r*)) nor the treasure of 'Uthman.
You have no spiritual connection whatsoever with your ancestors.

وہ زمانے میں معـــــزز تھے مسلماں ہو کر
اور تم خوار ہوئے تارکِ قرآں ہو کر

Woh Zamane Mein Mu'azzaz The Musalman Ho Kar
Aur Tum Khawar Huwe Taarik-e-Quran Ho Kar

They were honored in this world because they were Muslims.
You are disgraced today because you have forsaken the Qur'an.

◌ ◌ ◌

Stanza (21)

تم ہو آپس میں غضب ناک وہ آپس میں رحیم ۔ تم خطاکار و خطابیں وہ خطا پوش و کریم

Tum Ho Apas Mein Ghazabnak, Woh Apas Mein
Raheem
Tum Khatakaar-o-Khatabeen, Woh Khata Posh-o-
Kareem

You are irate at each other and they were mutually
compassionate.
You are sinners, measuring the sins of others, while
they were generous, hiding the errors of others.

چاہتے سب میں کہ ہوں اوجِ ثریا پہ مقیم ۔ پہلے ویسا کوئی پیدا تو کرے قلبِ سلیم

Chahte Sub Hain Ke Hon Auj-e-Surayya Pe Muqeem,
Pehle Waisa Koi Paida Tho Kare Qalb-e-Salim!

Everybody has the desire to occupy a seat on the peak
of Paradise,
But has anybody developed the pristine heart to
deserve it?

تختِ فغفور بھی ان کا تھا سریر بھی

یونہی باتیں ہیں کہ تم میں وہ حمیت ہے بھی؟

Takht-e-Faghfoor Bhi Un Ka Tha, Sareer-e-Ke Bhi
Yunhi Baatain Hain Ke Tum Mein Woh Hameeyyat
Hai Bhi?

They occupied the throne of China and the crown of
Iran.
Known only for your boasting words, do you have the
kind of self-esteem they had?

∽ ∽ ∽

Stanza (22)

خودکشی شیوہ تمھارا، وہ غیور و خوددار   تم اخوت سے گریزاں، وہ اخوت پہ نثار

Khudkushi Shewa Tumhara, Woh Ghayoor-o-Khuddar
Tum Akhuwat Se Gurezan, Woh Akhuwat Pe Nisar

You are on a suicide course, while they were known
for their pride and high self-esteem.
You are wary of brotherhood, while they preferred it
to their lives.

تم ہو گفتار سراپا، وہ سراپا کردار   تم ترستے ہو کلی کو، وہ گلستاں بہ کنار

Tum Ho Guftar Sarapa, Woh Sarapa Kirdar
Tum Taraste Ho Kali Ko, Woh Gulistan Bah Kinar

74

You are nothing but a stock of words, while they were men of perfect character.

You are seen begging for one flower, while they had vast gardens under their possession.

اب تلک یاد ہے قوموں کو حکایت اُن کی
نقش ہے صفحۂ ہستی پہ صداقت اُن کی

Ab Talak Yaad Hai Qoumon Ko Hikayat Un Ki
Naqsh Hai Safah-e-Hasti Pe Sadaqat Un Ki

Till date, nations remember the lessons taught by them.

Stories of their honesty are embedded in the history of the world.

∾ ∾ ∾

Stanza (23)

مثلِ انجم اُفقِ قوم پہ روشن بھی ہوئے   بتِ ہندی کی محبت میں برہمن بھی ہوئے

Misl-e-Anjum Ufaq-e-Qoum Pe Roshan Bhi Huwe
Buth-e-Hindi Ki Mohabbat Mein Barhman Bhi Huwe

Like a star you became radiant on the horizon of your nation.

Later, lured by the love of the Indian idols, you became Brahmins.

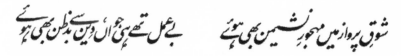

Shauq-e-Parwaz Mein Mehjoor-e-Nasheman Bhi Huwe
Be-Amal Thai Hi Jawan, Deen-e-Se Badzan Bhi Huwe

In your passion to fly, you lost your nest.
Devoid of noble deeds, your youth became skeptics.

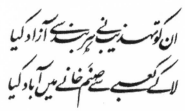

In Ko Tehzeeb Ne Har Bande Se Azad Kiya
La Ke Kaabe Se Sanamkhane Mein Abad Kiya

The modern civilization has freed them from all noble bonds.

It has dragged them away from Ka'bah and settled them in the temple of idols.

Stanza (24)

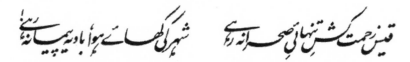

Qais Zehmat Kash-e-Tanhai-e-Sehra Na Rahe
Shehr Ki Khaye Huwa, Bad Ye Pema Na Rahe!

Qays is no longer able to bear the hardships of the
loneliness in the desert.
Having tasted the urban winds, he is no longer able to
roam.

Woh To Diwana Hai, Basti Mein Rahe Ya Na Rahe
Ye Zaroori Hai Hijab-e-Rukh-e-Laila Na Rahe!

He is insane, whether in town or not.
The face of Layla should never be invisible to him.

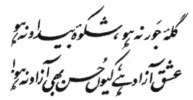

Gila-e-Jor Na Ho, Shikwa-e-Baidad Na Ho
Ishq Azad Hai, Kyun Husn Bhi Azad Na Ho!

77

Never complain of oppression and never lament about tyranny.

While love knows no bonds, why should beauty not be free?

∾ ∾ ∾

Stanza (25)

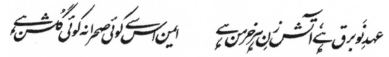

Ehd-e-Nau Barq Hai, Aatish Zan-e-Har Khirman Hai
Ayman Is Se Koi Sehra Na Koi Gulshan Hai

The modern age is a bolt that sets every nest on fire.
No forest and no garden is safe from its rage.

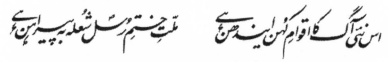

Is Nayi Aag Ka Aqwam-e-Kuhan Indhan Hai
Millat-e-Khatam-e-Rusal (s) Shaola Ba Perahan Hai

The fire of the new age is consuming the old nations as its fuel.
The cloak of the community of the final Messenger (s) has caught fire.

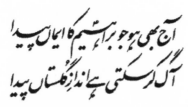

Aaj Bhi Ho Jo Baraheem (a.s) Ka Imaan Paida
Aag Kar Sakti Hai Andaz-e-Gulistan Paida

If the kind of faith that Ibrahim (*a.s*) had is revived today,
Fire too can produce the comfort of the garden.

ॐ ॐ ॐ

Stanza (26)

Dekh Kar Rang-e-Chaman Ho Na Pareshan Mali
Koukab-e-Ghuncha Se Shakhain Hain Chamakne Wali

Let the gardener not be sad at the plight of the garden.
Bunches of flowers will bloom from the buds, and
branches will shine.

Khas-o-Khashaak Se Hota Hai Gulistan Khali
Gul Bar Andaaz Hai Khoon-e-Shuhada Ki Laali

Withered leaves and weeds do spoil the garden,
But once again the red blood of the martyrs will colour
the roses.

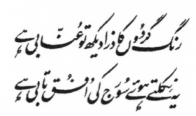

Rang Gardoon Ka Zara Dekh Tho Unnabi Hai
Yeh Nikalte Huwe Suraj Ki Ufaq Taabi Hai

Look at the bright colour on the horizon of the skies.
That in fact is the glow of the rising sun.

❧ ❧ ❧

Stanza (27)

Ummatain Gulshan-e-Hasti Mein Samar Cheeda Bhi
Hain
Aur Mehroom-e-Samar Bhi Hain, Khazan Didah Bhi
Hain

Some nations in this age-old garden of life have
enjoyed its fruits.
Some remain deprived of these fruits, and some others
have seen only the winter.

سیکڑوں نخل ہیں کا ہیدہ بھی بالیدہ بھی ہیں   سیکڑوں بطن چمن میں ابھی پوشیدہ بھی ہیں

Saikdon Nakhl Hain, Kaheeda Bhi, Baleeda Bhi Hain
Saikdon Batan-e-Chaman Mein Abhi Poshida Bhi Hain

There are trees in hundreds. Some are decayed and
some are robust,
And there are many more that still remain hidden
beneath the soil.

نخل اسلام نمونہ ہے بروسندی کا

پھل ہے یہ سیکڑوں صدیوں کی چمن بندی کا

Nakhl-e-Islam Namoona Hai Bru-Mandi Ka
Phal Hai Ye Saikdon Saalon Ki Chaman Bandi Ka

The tree of Islam is a sample of resurgence.
It is in fact the fruit of careful nourishing, down the
millennium.

∾ ∾ ∾

Stanza (28)

پاک ہے گردِ وطن سے سرِ دامان تیرا ٭ تُو وہ یوسف ہے کہ ہر مصر ہے کنعاں تیرا

Pak Hai Gard-e-Watan Se Sirr-e-Daman Tera
Thu Woh Yusaf Hai Ke Har Misr Hai Kinaan Tera

The dust of nationalism has not tainted the corner of
your robe.
You are like Yusuf and hence every Egypt for you is a
Kan'an of your own.

قافلہ ہو نہ سکے گا کبھی ویراں تیرا ٭ غیر یک بانگِ درا کچھ نہیں ساماں تیرا

Qafila Ho Na Sake Ga Kabhi Weeran Tera
Ghair Yak Bang-e-Dara Kuch Nahin Saman Tera

Your convoy will never get dispersed.
You need only the marching order and not any
baggage.

نخلِ شمع استی و در شعلہ دوَد ریشۂ تو ٭ عاقبت سوز بوَد سایۂ اندیشۂ تو

Nakhl-e-Shama Asti-o-Dar Shola Dawad Resha-e-Tu
Aaqbat Soz Bawad Saya-e-Andesha-e-Tu

You are a candle whose top is kept burning by the thread that emerges from its bottom.
The shade of your thoughts will illuminate all the future times.

Stanza (29)

تو نہ مٹ جائے گا ایران کے مٹ جانے سے نشۂ مے کو تعلق نہیں پیمانے سے

Tu Na Mit Jaye Ga Iran Ke Mit Jane Se
Nasha-e-Mai Ko Ta'aluq Nahin Pemane Se

You will not disappear if Iran goes down.
The pot of wine has nothing to do with the impact of the wine.

ہے عیاں یورشِ تاتار کے افسانے سے پاسباں مل گئے کعبے کو صنم خانے سے

Hai Ayan Yorish-e-Tataar Ke Afsane Se
Pasban Mil Gaye Kaabe Ko Sanam Khane Se

It is evident from the tales of the onslaught of the Mongols
The Ka'bah gets its custodians even from the abodes of the idols.

کشتیِ حق کا زمانے میں سہارا تُو ہے
عصرِ نُو رات ہے دُھندلا سا ستارا تُو ہے

Kashti-e-Haq Ka Zamane Mein Sahara Tu Hai
Asr-e-Nau Raat Hai, Dhundla Sa Sitara Tu Hai

In the world today the fleet of truth depends on you.
The modern age is a dark night and you are the dim pole
star.

෧ ෧ ෧

Stanza (30)

ہے جو ہنگامہ بپا یورشِ بلغاری کا ‌ غافلوں کے لیے پیغام ہے بیداری کا

Hai Jo Hangama Bipa Yorish-e-Balghari Ka
Ghafilon Ke Liye Pegham Hai Baidari Ka

There is an uproar about the onslaught of the
Bulgarian forces.
That in fact is a call for those in slumber to wake up.

تُو سمجھتا ہے یہ ساماں ہے دلِ آزاری کا ‌ امتحاں ہے ترے ایثار کا، خودداری کا

Tu Samajhta Hai Ye Saman Hai Dil Aazari Ka
Imtihan Hai Tere Isaar Ka, Khud-Dari Ka

Do you look at it as a cause of grief for you?
That in fact is a test of your pride and your spirit of
sacrifice.

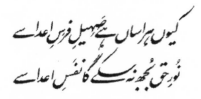

Kyun Harasan Hai Saheel-e-Faras-e-Aada Se
Noor-e-Haq Bujh Na Sake Ga Nafs-e-Aada Se

Why are you so scared of the might of your foes?
The torch of truth can never be put out by their blows.

ॐ ॐ ॐ

Stanza (31)

Chashme-e-Aqwam Se Makhfi Hai Haqiqat Theri
Hai Abhi Mehfil-e-Hasti Ko Zaroorat Theri

The truth about you is hidden from the eyes of the
nations across the globe.
The sphere of existence needs you today more than ever.

85

زندہ رکھتی ہے زمانے کو حرارت تیری کوکب قسمت امکاں ہے خلافت تیری

Zinda Rakhti Hai Zamane Ko Hararat Teri
Koukab-e-Qismat-e-Imkan Hai Khilafat Teri

It is your warmth that keeps the world alive.
Your *khilafah* is the star of hope for great prospects.

وقت فرصت ہے کہاں، کام ابھی باقی ہے نورِ توحید کا اتمام ابھی باقی ہے

Waqt-e-Fursat Hai Kahan, Kaam Abhi Baqi Hai
Noor-e-Touheed Ka Itmam Abhi Baqi Hai

With the mission waiting to be accomplished, you have no time to relax.
The task of spreading the light of unity has not been fulfilled till date.

෧ ෧ ෧

Stanza (32)

مثل بو قید ہے غنچے میں پریشاں ہو جا رخت بردوش ہوا اے چمنستاں ہو جا

Misl-e-Bu Qaid Hai Ghunche Mein, Pareshan Ho Ja
Rakht Bar Dosh Hawaye Chamanistan Ho Ja

Like a fragrance, you are imprisoned right now in the
bud: Reach out.
Ride over the breeze and make the garden of earth
fragrant.

ہے تنگ مایہ تو ذرے سے بیاباں ہوجا   نغمہ موج سے ہنگامہ طوفان ہوجا!

Hai Tunk Maya To Zarre Se Byaban Ho Ja
Naghma-e-Mouj Se Hangama-e-Toofan Ho Ja!

You are worthless right now: Be a desert, not a mere
speck of sand.
No longer should you remain the music of the wave:
Make a thundering hurricane of yourself.

قوت عشق سے ہر پست کو بالا کر دے
دہر میں اسم محمد سے اجالا کر دے

Quwwat-e-Ishq Se Har Past Ko Bala Kar De
Dehr Mein Ism-e-Muhammad (s) Se Ujala Kar De

Through the strength of love, raise everything lying
low to great heights.

87

Make this world shine in the light of the name of
Muhammad (s).

❧ ❧ ❧

Stanza (33)

هو نہ یہ پھول تو بلبل کا ترنم بھی نہ ہو   چمنِ دہر میں کلیوں کا تبسم بھی نہ ہو

Ho Na Ye Phool To Bulbul Ka Tarannum Bhi Na Ho
Chaman-e-Dehr Mein Kaliyon Ka Tabassum Bhi Na
Ho

If these flowers do not exist, you will never hear the
songs of the bulbul.
Smiles of the rose buds too will never adorn the
garden.

یہ نہ ساقی ہو تو پھرے مے بھی نہ ہو خم بھی نہ ہو   بزمِ توحید بھی دنیا میں نہ ہو، تم بھی نہ ہو

Ye Na Saqi Ho To Phir Mai Bhi Na Ho, Khum Bhi Na Ho
Bazm-e-Touheed Bhi Dunya Mein Na Ho, Tum Bhi Na
Ho

And if this server of wine ceases to exist, there will
remain neither the wine nor its effect.
The glory of unity will vanish and you will vanish too.

خیمۂ افلاک کا استادہ اسی نام سے ہے
نبضِ ہستی تپش آمادہ اسی نام سے ہے

Khema Aflak Ka Istada Issi Naam Se Hai
Nabz-e-Hasti Tapish Aamadah Issi Naam Se Hai

That name of His is the foundation the skies stand on.
The pulse of existence is live and warm thanks to that
name.

ᘒ ᘒ ᘒ

Stanza (34)

دشت میں دامنِ کہسار میں میدان میں ہے   بحر میں موج کی آغوش میں طوفان میں ہے

Dasht Mein, Daman-e-Kuhsar Mein, Maidan Mein
Hai
Behr Mein, Mouj Ki Aghosh Mein, Toofan Mein Hai

That name is in the forests, tranquil hills, plains,
Seas, bosom of the waves and the hurricanes.

چین کے شہر مراقش کے بیابان میں ہے   اور پوشیدہ مسلمان کے ایمان میں ہے

89

Cheen Ke Shehr, Maraqash Ke Byaban Mein Hai
Aur Poshida Musalman Ke Iman Mein Hai

It is in the towns of China and wilds of Morocco,
And is hidden in the faith of the Muslim.

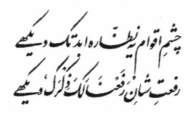

Chashm-e-Aqwam Ye Nazara Abad Tak Dekhe
Riffat-e-Shan-e-'Rafaana La Ka Zikrak' Dekhe

Let the eyes of the nations always watch this milieu.
Let them glance at the great glory of "And We raised
high for you your repute."[3]

∾ ∾ ∾

Stanza (35)

Mardam-e-Chashm-e-Zameen Yani Woh Kali Dunya
Woh Tumhare Shuhada Palne Wali Dunya

---

3. Qur'an 94:4.

Men of that pupil of the earth or that dark continent of the world (Africa),
The world that nourishes your martyrs.

گرمیِ مہر کی پروردہ ہلالی دنیا ۔۔۔ عشق والے جسے کہتے ہیں بلالی دنیا

Garmi-e-Mehr Ki Parwarda Hilali Dunya
Ishq Wale Jise Kehte Hain Bilali Dunya

The land that looks like the new moon, nurtured by the warmth of the sun,
People of love call the land of Bilal.

تپش اندوز ہے اس نام سے پارے کی طرح
غوطہ زن نور میں ہے آنکھ کے تارے کی طرح

Tapish Andoz Hai Iss Naam Se Paare Ki Tarah
Ghouta Zan Noor Mein Hai Aankh Ke Tare Ki Tarah

It gets warmed up and moves like mercury when that name is mentioned.
It dives deep into the pool of light like the pupil of the eye.

ɷ ɷ ɷ

Stanza (36)

عقل ہے تیری سپر عشق ہے شمشیر تری   مرے درویش! خلافت ہے جہانگیر تری

Aqal Hai Teri Sipar, Ishq Hai Shamsheer Teri
Mere Darvaish! Khilafat Hai Jahangeer Teri

Wisdom is your shield and love is your sword.
My dervish, your vicegerency covers the entire universe.

ماسوئی اللہ کے لیے آگ ہے تکبیر تری   تو مسلماں ہو تو تقدیر ہے تدبیر تری

Ma Siwa Allah Ke Liye Aag Hai Takbeer Teri
Tu Musalman Ho To Taqdeer Hai Tadbeer Teri

Your *takbir* is fire for everything except Allah. Become a
Muslim and each plan of yours will be your destiny.

کی محمدؐ سے وفا تو نے تو ہم تیرے ہیں
یہ جہاں چیز ہے کیا لوح و قلم تیرے ہیں

Ki Muhammad (s) Se Wafa Tu Ne Tho Hum There Hain
Yeh Jahan Cheez Hai Kya, Loh-o-Qalam There Hain

Remain loyal to Muhammad (s) and
We shall belong to you.
Let alone this meagre world, the book and pen of destiny
will all be yours.

Made in the USA
Las Vegas, NV
06 September 2021

29728563R00062